WHITE

A revisea
presented at the Shaw Theatre, 1976

by

PETER SHAFFER

SAMUEL   FRENCH

LONDON
NEW YORK TORONTO SYDNEY HOLLYWOOD

WHITE LIARS

This revised version was first presented by the Dolphin
Theatre Company at the Shaw Theatre, London, on
June 29th, 1976, with the following cast of characters:

Sophie, Baroness Lemberg	Maggie Fitzgibbon
Frank	Peter Machin
Tom	Timothy Dalton

Directed by Paul Giovanni

The action takes place in the Fortune Teller's Parlour
of Sophie, Baroness Lemberg, on the pier of a run-down
seaside resort on the south coast of England

Time—the present

WHITE LIARS

The Fortune Teller's Parlour of Sophie, Baroness Lemberg, on the pier of a run-down seaside resort on the south coast of England. Around 5 p.m., late September

Sophie's parlour is set between two levels of the pier. It is reached from above by an iron staircase, and it is set on iron stanchions rising out of the sea. As we look at it, it seems to be suspended against the wet five o'clock sky: a cluttered nest in a tangle of Victorian ironwork. The room is actually divided by a curtain into two: a little ante-room, with a bench for waiting; and the consulting-room, which is much larger, and is replete with a covered table on a rotting strip of carpet, and a couple of broken-down chairs. On the table stands the faded photograph of a middle-aged man, in an ornate silver frame. A completed game of patience is laid out on the cloth. On a shelf at the back stands the crystal-ball, under a covering. The window, streaked with salt and bird-droppings, proclaims in reverse gilt letters: "BARONESS LEMBERG. PALMISTE. CLAIRVOYANTE". And in smaller letters underneath: "LEMBERG NEVER LIES". The place is dirty and claustrophobic, deriving its mystery from the fantasy of its location, hung over the water. Little light bulbs are festooned down the pier, above

As the CURTAIN *rises and the Lights come up through the cobweb of rusty iron, we see Sophie standing at her table, carefully pouring gin from a half-bottle through a funnel into a rose-coloured decanter. She is a woman of fifty, once beautiful and still handsome, dressed in the blouse and skirt of a professional working woman. When she speaks her voice is marked by a strong but never incomprehensible German accent. She drops the bottle into a waste-basket, picks up a delicate little rose-coloured wineglass and pours some gin into it. Seagulls suddenly scream. She raises her glass to them*

Sophie *Salut!* Bloody things! Greedy, filthy, middle-class birds. Here's to you! And to another brilliant, dazzling afternoon in

Grinmouth-on-Sea! Grinmouth, glorious Grinmouth—Fairy-
land of the South Coast! (*She swallows her gin*) You know
something, I think they're watering the drink in this country.
This is definitely less fortifying than it used to be. But that
of course is no surprise. It is one of the iron laws of life: everything gets less fortifying. What Goes Down Must Go Downer!
Lemberg's Law of Life . . .! (*She turns to the photograph.
Imploringly, like a little girl*) Oh, don't look so disapproving,
please. What else am I going to do? Improve my mind for
the glittering society of Grinmouth-on-Sea? Look at it! (*She
goes to the window*) Not one gleam of sunlight for ten days.
Not one soul out walking, jetty to jetty. Nothing but wet
sand—rusty iron—plastic bottles all along the shore, and bird-
shit on the windows. I'm sorry for the language, Papa, but
there it is: see for yourself. *Vogeldrecke* on every pane: who
needs curtains? And the sea. This ravishing sea! Look at it,
if you please—such an exotic colour. It's exactly like they've
poured out ten million cups of tea. No wonder they call it the
English Channel! Grinmouth-on-*Tea*, that's what I name it
from now on. (*She laughs sourly*) You hear that, Papa?
That's my joke for today. Grinmouth-on-Tea! I admit it's not
one of my best. But then *you* sit here all day entirely by yourself, you're not going to win Decorations for your wit either!
(*She pours some more gin, and gulps*) The truth is, my dear,
they haven't the faintest idea what water should look like
in this country. Do you remember our lake? Our beautiful
summer lake, what it was like to come back to each year?
Clear, clear water—absolutely still—with the pine trees standing in it, upside down—how was it you called them?—rows
of little green soldiers marching on their heads! You had
really a good power of description you know, sometimes . . .
(*She sits at her table*) Beloved God, this silence! You'd think
someone would consult me, if only to ask should they kill
themselves. Do you realize there hasn't been an actual human
being in this room for six days? And then it was only Mr
Fowler with his boring Rent Book. (*Imitating a "common"
accent*) "I hate to mention it, Baroness, but you owe us more
than a little back rent!" More than a little! Only six bloody
weeks! "Hate to mention it"—he loves it: boring old swine!
Sorry, Papa, your Sophie is getting just a little bad tempered

with the world. Can you really blame her? How would *you* like it to sit here all day in this black little prison, with draughts going up *your* skirts. I'm sorry, I mean trousers! (*She giggles*) Excuse me, Father—you are absolutely right. A lady shouldn't drink. Though actually, I don't know why. I was under the impression, my dear, that the aristocracy set the Do's and Don'ts, not followed them. That is entirely for the middle classes . . . (*She looks up and out*) Beloved God, I don't believe it.

Frank and Tom appear on the upper level

Two whole clients! Oh God, oh my God! . . .

Frank and Tom lounge down the iron stairs and stand outside her window, apparently debating whether to come in. She watches them hungrily

Two pounds if they take the cards. Four if they take the crystal-ball! Beloved God, make them come in!

The two boys start to walk away

Come in, oh *please*!

They turn back and enter the ante-room

Tom Anyone home?
Sophie One moment, please!

She scurries about during the following, stacking the cards, getting the crystal-ball and setting it on the table, and adjusting her hair. Finally, she swirls around herself a grand-coloured shawl, sits and opens a fan! Of the two boys, Frank is middle-class, soft-spoken and gentle; his manner is shy, warm, and immediately likeable—in great contrast to his companion, who seems casual almost to the point of brutality. Tom is dressed very fancily, in bright colours, wears his hair long, and lounges about. He speaks in a heavy North country accent

Frank I'll go first.
Tom Why?
Frank I've got to get back to the Hall. I want to check that sound system.

Tom Why bother? There's not going to be an audience anyway.

Frank And whose fault is that?

Tom What d'you mean?

Frank We wouldn't be here at all, if it wasn't for your stupid astrologer.

Tom He's not stupid.

Frank "Avoid the seaside in the month of August." What d'you call *that*?

Tom Don't mock what you don't understand.

Frank All right, all right. I don't know what I'm doing with you anyway. You don't need a business manager. Why not just hire yourself a crack astrologer, and get him to fix all your engagements for you. He could make sure we'd go broke inside a month.

Tom (*surlily*) Shut up, will you?

Frank What are you going to ask *her* now? Where we play next?

Tom I said, shut up.

Frank (*appeasingly*) Look, Tom—I'm not mocking. You've got a right to believe what you please. But really this—this stuff can go too far sometimes. A two-year-old baby could tell you you don't play the seaside in late bloody September. If we'd come here six weeks ago, when they *wanted* us, we'd have cleaned up, and you know it.

Sophie (*calling*) Come in, please!

Frank I'm sorry but that's the truth. Astrology or no astrology!

Tom brushes by him into the Consulting Room. Frank follows him quickly. Sophie is seated regally at her table

Sophie Good evening. One of you at a time, please.

Tom (*dismissing Frank*) Right. I'll see you, then.

Frank (*standing his ground*) I—well, why don't we toss for it?

Tom (*surprised at being challenged*) Toss?

Frank Well, that's fair, isn't it?

Tom shrugs sullenly. Frank pulls a coin from his pocket

Well, it is . . . (*To Sophie, with a nervous laugh*) We're both so anxious to see you, it's a bit of a fight. (*To Tom*) Heads or tails?

Tom Heads.

Frank tosses

Frank Tails! I win! (*Showing it to Sophie*) True?

Sophie nods in acquiescence

(*To Tom*) Look, why don't you go for a ride on the dodgems? They'll be glad of the custom.

Tom shrugs again

Sophie Come back in ten minutes, please. Expert divination does not take very long.
Frank You don't mind, do you?
Tom You won, didn't you?

Tom lounges out

Frank looks after him

Sophie Come along, then.
Frank (*staring out of the window*) It's a rotten old day, isn't it? There isn't a soul out on the prom. Just us and the seagulls. They're all sitting in those little shelters meant for people.
Sophie Like rows of people from a sanitarium, coughing into their coat collars.
Frank That's a nasty thought.
Sophie It's a nasty place, mister. It makes you have nasty ideas.

He turns to look at her

Frank It must feel strange living with the sea all around you.
Sophie It is not a sea at all. It is merely a gutter between here and France. All the same, I prefer it to the land. A third-rate holiday resort is not my idea of a place to reside in . . . I have known other days, mister.
Frank I'd assumed that, of course.
Sophie You had? Why?
Frank From your manner. It's very—distinguished. And also of course from—well, your title.
Sophie I am a Baroness of the Holy Roman Empire. I was born with certain powers. Owing to an alteration in my fortune, I am reduced to selling these for money. It is regrettable, but then so is most of contemporary life . . . You have a

special purpose in coming to see me. Please tell me what it is, and don't waste my time.

Frank A special purpose?

Sophie Of course.

Frank How do you know?

Sophie That wasn't tails, mister.

Frank What?

Sophie The coin. It wasn't tails. It was heads.

Frank (*grinning nervously*) Oh . . . Yes, yes—yes—that's right. I know. I'm sorry about that. But I—I—I had to see you first. I really had . . . It's vital.

Sophie Ja?

Frank (*very ill at ease*) When we drove into town this morning in the van, I saw your sign right away. It says "Advice and Consultation". It sort of gave me the idea. Well, it gave me hope, actually.

Sophie Go on.

Frank I don't know. It seemed like a good idea, then. Now it's perfectly ridiculous. I mean, just embarrassing, really . . . The thing is, you mustn't be angry.

Sophie Angry?

Frank At what I'm going to ask. Promise that, please. You see, I've—I've got a suggestion. A sort of a—little game. A well, frankly a . . . Look, Baroness, I don't really want my fortune told at all. I've come about something entirely different. And you've every right to throw me out, and be very annoyed. Only I hope you won't be.

Sophie Young mister: I have no idea what you are saying. Am I supposed to be clairvoyant, or something? That's my joke. I often make it.

Frank Oh . . . Yes . . .

Sophie Sit down for a start. Come—come.

Frank sits

You're very pale. Are you ill?

Frank No.

Sophie Worried?

Frank Yes.

Sophie Is it your professional life?

Frank No. Look, I'll pay you, just like it was a regular session.

Actually, I thought I'd offer you a little more. Unless you'd be insulted.

Sophie Why should I be insulted? Advice is as hard as divination. It is your love life? Trouble with a girl? Ha?

Frank shrugs

Of course. And your friend is involved also. Ja, ja, ja . . .

Frank A bit cliché, isn't it?

Sophie It is not exactly unfamiliar, I admit. Two friends in love with the same girl.

Frank Except he's *not* in love with her. And she just thinks she's in love with him. She's very easily impressed. Mind you, I see in a way. He's an impressive boy. Susan's always been surrounded by phonies. Suddenly, along comes someone who's completely himself—it's bound to be a turn-on.

Sophie A what?

Frank It's bound to excite her.

Sophie This boy is working-class, ja?

Frank He could hardly be more so.

Sophie And the girl is not?

Frank You're clever, Baroness. You see things. Sue's bugbear is respectability. Her dad is a nice respectable department manager in John Lewis's. He's got himself a nice, respectable house in Chislehurst, and she's had enough golf and gardening to last her a lifetime. Tom represents everything her parents hate. Rotten slum background. Independence of the kind that really makes them nervous. The kind you can only have when you've truly had nothing to begin with. They'd call it arrogance. Well, you've seen him. He *is* arrogant, of course, he is. He's also extraordinary. (*Pause*) The trouble with me is, I see everyone's point of view. Here I am, defending him already.

Sophie This boy is an entertainer?

Frank Singer. Thanks to me. I found him singing in an East End pub, flat broke. A natural musician. I mean really marvellous. And with absolutely no idea what to do with it. I made a. whole group for him. That's my thing, you see: I'm a Manager, No point in being modest about it. If he's a natural singer. I'm a natural Manager. I created The Liars especially for him

Sophie The Liars?

Frank The White Liars. Four instrumentalists and Tom. I even designed the uniform. White satin—it's wild! Susan helped me, of course.

Sophie She helps you a lot, your girl?

Frank I don't know what I'd do without her. She does everything. Drives the van, does the accounts, nursemaids the boys —you'll meet her tonight, if you like. We're doing a show at the Winter Garden. Perhaps you'd like to come.

Sophie Thank you, no. As far as I'm concerned, the birth of electricity meant the death of music.

Frank (*laughing politely*) That's good.

Sophie It's not good, mister. It's true. There is no music made today: just noise.

Frank If you say so, Baroness.

Sophie Don't condescend to me, please. I come from the one country that created all the music that matters! And I was brought up to *listen* to it, my dear mister. Not just bob my head, or twist my tummy. My father was a *real* natural musician! He was an amateur in the true meaning of the word. Do you know what that means? A lover! He played the clarinet like a lover! It is hard to appreciate amateurs in the other sense of the word—bricklayers and plumbers hitting guitars, when one has known the Rosé.

Frank Rosé?

Sophie The Rosé String Quartet. No doubt you've never heard of them. Before the war they were the finest chamber players in Austria. My father knew them intimately. He would invite them each summer to our villa in the country, to play with him. And they would come. "Sir," they'd say, "it is an honour to play with someone as good as you!" They would all sit by the lake, by this glorious lake on our beautiful little private estate, and they would play together—the Brahms Quintet, in B Minor. I would always be the guest of honour. Ten, eleven, twelve years old, they'd put me in the middle of them, on a special armchair carried out on to the grass, and I would sit *engulfed* in the music! Sentimental, ja? Well, other years— other tears.

Frank It sounds marvellous.

Sophie My father was a man of great style. It is a way of conduct that has passed entirely from the world.

Frank (*looking at the photograph*) Is that him there?

Sophie It is.

Frank What are those things he's wearing?

Sophie (*loftily: not looking at the picture herself*) You mean decorations. The top one is the Order of St Michael. Next the Golden Spur. Last the papal medal of the Holy Roman Empire. Impressive, ja? As you would say—wow!

Frank Is he still alive?

Sophie No. He drowned.

Frank Drowned?

Sophie Ja: in middle-class mediocrity. When the Nazis came, we left Austria. What else could we do? As he observed, no man of civilization could continue to live there. Besides, my mother was of Romany blood. It was from her I derive my gift. Her mother had been a noblewoman of that very ancient race— but of course to the Nazis the Romanys were simply degenerates. We lived together all three in London. My father tried to work, but he'd been trained for nothing practical. All his life he'd been a diplomat—and the new Government detested him. The Third Reich only had use for traitors, of course. And so he passed his time mostly sitting by himself in Regent's Park, reading music scores, whilst first my mother and then I, after she'd taught me properly, practised our gift of Divination . . . Other years, other tears. We were talking of your girl-friend. What is it you want of me? You love her, ja?

Frank Yes.

Sophie Very much?

Frank We've been together two years—and it's been the best time I've ever known.

Sophie But now it is ending?

Frank Not if I can help it.

Sophie Because of him? Your friend?

Frank Look, when I first met Tom he'd only been down from Yorkshire three weeks. He was living in a filthy little cellar in the slums. He was absolutely miserable.

Sophie So you took him into your house?

Frank The stupidest thing I ever did. I gave him a room in my flat, free. The thing about Tom is, he's a monster. I mean that in the Greek way. Like one of those things in a fable. He *lives* on worship. It's his food. I mean it quite literally: he can hardly get through a day without two tablespoons of sticky golden worship poured down his throat, preferably by a girl. Poor Sue walked right into it, you see. I mean because that's a bit her scene—spooning it out. And the awful thing is, she's getting more and more turned on. Every day I watch it happening. It's like I can't stop it. Any moment now she's going to cross that landing from our bedroom to his. I just know it.

Sophie So prevent it! Tell him to go!

Frank Well, that's it. I can't—I just can't. I'm just—incapable. Isn't that stupid? For one thing, it's just so corny—Keep Your Hands off My Girl! I mean he'd laugh. I'd just look so silly, you know, squaring up, losing my cool. I can't do that. It's not me. Anyway, it isn't that simple. The thing is, he's so bloody disarming. I can't explain really. I lie in bed at night beside her, rehearsing scenes I'm going to have with Tom in the morning. I make up whole conversations—brilliant cutting sentences—or maybe ones more in sorrow than in anger, you know, rather noble. And then in the daylight, I look at him and he's swabbing crusts round the egg yolk on his plate, and I just can't bring them out. I mean, people aren't in your head, are they? (*Pause*) The thing is, I can't take any more. He's got to get out! *I've got to get him out!*

His vehemence seems to surprise them both

   (*After a pause*) I had this wild idea.

Sophie What kind of idea?

Frank That you could—see it all.

Sophie See?

Frank In the ball.

Sophie (*slowly*) See all—what?

Frank (*getting nervous*) Look, the thing about Tom is—he's fantastically superstitious. I mean, ridiculous. He's always loping off to fortune-tellers and palmists, every place he goes. One week it's a woman in Acton who does it with beans. The next, it's some Chinaman in Clapham who does it with dice.

Sophie And now it's some German in Grinmouth who does it— with what exactly?

Frank Well, this, actually, I thought . . . (*He produces an envelope from his pocket*) The main facts of Tom's life. It's all

stuff he's told me over the past year. Yorkshire childhood—
coalmining village—drunken dad who threw his guitar on the
fire. They're pretty dismal, really. I thought——

Sophie What? That as I'm a fake, I could not possibly find them
out for myself?

Frank Of course not! Only using this, you'd be absolutely
accurate. I mean absolutely. So exact you'd have him freaked.
He'd totally believe you—totally: you can't imagine it. I
mean if you were to see something a bit . . .

Sophie Ja? A bit . . .?

Frank Alarming—in his future.

Sophie What kind of alarming, mister?

Frank Well, like some dangerous relationship.

Sophie With a girl.

Frank Yes.

Sophie Which, of course, he should break off immediately. If he
doesn't terrible disaster waits for him. Ja? (*Amused*) Blood and
calamity!

Frank It sounds ridiculous, I know. Like I said. With anyone
else but Tom it would be. But I swear to you, any kind of
warning coming from you—because you're very impressive,
you really are—he'd actually stop and think. It could work.

Sophie And how much am I to receive for this absurdity?

Frank I thought three pounds would be . . .

Sophie Suitable? (*Silence*) Mister, I know I don't look so pros-
perous here in this filthy, little room, but who do you think
I am? Some silly gypsy bitch in a caravan, you can buy for
three pounds?

Frank No, of course not.

Sophie (*with grandeur*) I practise here in this hideous town, an
art as old, as sacred as medicine. Look at this! (*She shoots out
her hand*) This hand has held the hand of a Royal Duchess
in intimate spiritual communion. It has held the hand of an
Archimandite—a Prince of the Orthodox Church, who said
to me, *bowing* to me, "Baroness, you are not just a fortune-
teller: you have the divine gift!" All right, I have—what is it?
—"*come down*" in the world! Come down to Grinmouth!
Down to Pizza stalls! and grease in the air! dodge them cars
and rifle guns and all the fun in the fairground! Every day
now—if I see nobody at all!—my *noble* clients are people

like old potatoes wearing paper hats saying "Kiss Me!" Whispering old spinsters, smelling of camphor—old red men with gin in their eyes, begging me to predict just one football pool to make them rich for life! *Rubbish people*, all of them, *killing* me to death with their middle-class dreams! But one thing, mister—I may hate them, but I never cheat them. Lemberg never lies!

A pause

Frank I'm sorry.
Sophie That's all right. Go now, please.

Frank crosses in silence through the curtain and into the ante-room. Sophie sits staring after him, clasping her hands together in anxiety

Sophie (*sotto voce*) Three pounds! Three pounds, three pounds, three whole pounds . . .!

Suddenly, Frank returns, abruptly

Frank Look, I really am sorry. It was disgusting to do that. I'm sorry: I see that now . . . But I'm desperate, Baroness. I love this girl. I'd do anything to keep her. Tom is ruthless. You can't understand that. Someone from your world couldn't possibly understand . . . I'm sorry. Good-bye. (*As abruptly, he makes to go again*)
Sophie (*stopping him*) One moment, please. (*A pause*) I misjudged you, mister. I thought you were like him. The two of you were together in my mind. I thought: tummy-twisters! Head-bobbers! No sensitivity or gentleness about them. But I was wrong . . . (*She rises*) I see after all you have a faithful nature. I have come to believe that faithfulness in love is like real music—one of the marvels of the past. It is good to find it still exists. Look, there he is: coming back!

We hear the sound of Tom's whistling. He comes into view on the upper level of the pier: in his hand is a large, woolly toy dog

Sophie and Frank watch him through the window, as he stands looking at the sea

Look at him. Ja: I see it now. What you said: the arrogance!
You're kind about him, because you are a kind man. Disarming, you call him. Well, mister, he doesn't disarm me. I see
what he is. I see them every day, the new savages. I watch
them on this pier, whistling up and down with their stupid
fuzzy hair, stumbling along in their stupid high shoes. Sequins
on their shoulders, pretending to be amusing and eccentric—
but really, underneath, just thugs! Working-class thugs! They
think they own the world. Ja, and we let them think it. *We*—
you and I—the foolish ones, the romantics, the *square* ones as
they see us. Well, for once one of *them* is going to get it.
(*Briskly*) I'll help you, mister. I'll keep your girl safe for you.
I'll frighten the sequins right off this little taker. Give me the
envelope.

*Sophie stretches out her hand for the envelope. Tom turns to the
stairs. Frank hesitates*

Quick, quick, quick, quick!

Frank hands it over

It will cost you ten pounds.

Frank Ten?!

Sophie Of course, ten. Do you think I compromise my art for
nothing? Take it or leave it.

Frank All right.

Tom comes down the stairs

Sophie Good, then! Sssssh, he's coming. Sit! Sit . . .!

Frank sits at the table. So does she

Now tell me quick, what colour is your girl?

Frank Blonde.

Sophie More.

Frank She usually wears a pink scarf round her head. She's very
fond of that. A pink scarf. You can see it in there—(*pointing
to the crystal ball*)—if you like.

Tom enters the ante-room

Sophie Ssssh!

*They freeze as **Tom** enters the ante-room*

(*Raising her voice*) And you, my dear, your dominant colour is green—your lucky day of the week is Wednesday, and, as I said before, everything in your cards indicates activity, activity and again activity! That will be two pounds, please.

Frank hands her ten pounds, very reluctantly. She counts them carefully

Sophie It's going to be a very busy year, believe me. Lemberg never lies.
Frank Well, thank you, Baroness.
Sophie Thank you. I wonder if your friend has returned.
Frank (*raising his voice*) Tom!
Tom Yeh.
Sophie Ah: good. Ask him to be kind enough to wait one minute, please. (*Indicating the envelope*) I'll call when I'm ready.
Frank Of course. Good-bye now.
Sophie Good-bye.
Frank (*for Tom's benefit, at the curtain*) And thank you again.

Frank goes through into the ante-room. Hastily, Sophie sits at the table, tears open the envelope and starts reading it

(*To Tom*) Hallo.
Tom (*sotto voce*) Well, how is she?

This ensuing scene is sotto voce

Frank She's—she's all right . . .
Tom What did she tell you?
Frank Nothing, actually . . . Actually, she's lousy.
Tom What d'you mean?
Sophie (*calling out*) One moment, mister, please! I'll be with you immediately! (*Reading the notes*) "Born nineteen fifty-three . . ." (*She writes it on her fan*)
Tom Is she really hopeless?
Frank Well, they're all fakes, aren't they?
Tom Of course they're not!
Frank Well, this one didn't get a thing right! If you ask me, they should cancel her Witch Licence.
Tom (*alarmed*) Sssh!
Frank Why?
Tom You mustn't call them that!

Sophie (*reading the notes: concentrating*)   "Mining village—father drunkard." (*She writes on her fan*)

Frank (*seeing the toy dog*) What the hell's that?

Tom I won it. There's a rifle stall by the turnstiles. They were so glad to see me, they virtually gave it to me. I'll give it Sue.

Frank He looks drunk to me.

Tom It's all that fresh air. It's knocked the poor bugger out!

Sophie (*to the photograph, sotto voce*) Why are you staring at me? It's ten pounds, that's all that matters . . . And anyway, surely, it is a major duty of the aristocracy to give lessons when necessary. (*She turns the photograph away from her and takes another drink, knocking it back*)

Tom What's she doing in there? Is she in a trance or something?

Frank I don't know. I think she calls it preparing.

Tom You mean like meditation. It probably is.

Frank I bet she's just taking a quick zizz, poor old cow!

Tom (*furious*) Ssssh! I *told* you!

Sophie (*reading the notes*) "Boxing Day—ran away from home—Boxing Day." (*She writes it on her fan*)

Frank (*in sudden panic*) Look—why don't you just come back with me?

Tom What for?

Frank Because it really is a waste of money. This *one* is!

Tom (*slyly*) Here—there's nothing funny about her, is there? Are you sure she didn't tell you something?

Frank Nothing, not a damn thing!

Tom Well, you look a bit funny to me.

Frank I'm bored, that's all. I'm just plain bored! You'll hate it!

Sophie (*reading*) "Pink scarf . . ."

Tom Well, I'm here now, and she's seen me, so I might as well go in.

Frank Tom, listen to me!

Sophie (*calling out*) I'm ready, mister. Enter, please! (*Reading the last note again, and putting away the envelope*) "Pink scarf—pink scarf . . ."

Tom (*to Frank*) I'll see you back there.

Frank All right. Don't say I didn't warn you . . .

Tom (*setting the dog on him*) Arf! Arf! Arf! You just go and check that sound system.

Tom chucks the dog on a chair, and lounges into the Parlour. Frank lingers for a second

Sophie Come in, mister. Sit down . . .

Tom stays by the curtain—turns and lifts it, to find Frank still there

Tom (*coldly, to Frank*) Did I eavesdrop on *you*?

Frank leaves in confusion. He goes up the iron stairs and off out of sight

Tom lets the curtain fall, and approaches the table where Sophie sits waiting

Sophie So. Here is my scale of charges. (*She hands him a card*) Two pounds for cards alone. Two pounds fifty, cards and palms. Three pounds for the crystal-ball. I recommend the ball. It is more profound.

Tom (*agreeing*) Yeh.

Sophie You're an addict, I think.

Tom Addict? You mean drugs?

Sophie Divination. You go often to consult people.

Tom (*surprised*) That's right, actually. Does it show?

Sophie You have comparing eyes.

Tom Oh. That's no fun, is it?

Sophie (*coldly*) They don't disturb me, mister. When you are older, you will learn that you can't go *shopping* in the world of the occult. People with the Gift do not live in Supermarkets, you know. Give me something you wear, please. Your scarf will do . . .

Warily he hands her his scarf

Thank you. Now please sit.

He sits

And we begin. (*She takes the cover off the ball*) There. Just a ball of glass. Except that nothing is *just* anything.

Tom Of course not.

Sophie (*abruptly*) Sssh! Don't speak, please. (*She puts his scarf on the ball*) You are a musician.

Tom nods delightedly

   (*Sarcastically*) It's not such an amazing guess, mister. I've just finished reading your friend, after all. I hope he was satisfied.

Tom Oh . . . Yes . . .

Sophie He has good emanations. He is going to have a very happy domestic life.

Tom Yeh?

Sophie (*hostile*) Yeh. (*She stares at him. A pause*) We begin now. What month were you born?

Tom May.

Sophie Taurus. Impetuous. Sometimes ruthless.

Tom Twenty-fifth.

Sophie Gemini. Interesting. (*She removes the handkerchief and peers savagely into the ball*) It's very disturbed. Much confusion. Nineteen fifty-three. You were born in nineteen fifty-three.

Tom (*amazed*) Yes!

Sophie It's ritualistic, the ball. Often it gives first the date of birth, then the place. Ja, exactly. Now I see a house—a little narrow house in a dirty street. At the end a huge wheel turning in the sky. A coal-wheel!—a coal-village . . . I see I'm not too far from the truth.

Tom can only nod, speechless. Covertly she consults her fan for more details, and goes on peering into the ball

   There is no woman in the house. Your mother is dead, ja? Your father, still alive. At least I see a man in working-clothes. A bad face. Brutal face. Thick like a drunken man.

They exchange stares. Tom is very disturbed

   And now? I see a child. A little pale face. Eyes of fear, looking here—there—for escape. Such a frightened face. He ill-treated you, this father? He beat you?

Tom rises and begins to pace about

   What is this now? A fire. Something burning on it—it looks like a guitar.

He turns on her, startled

   Can that be right, a guitar? What is that? Some symbol of your music talent?

Tom No . . .

Sophie I disturb you, mister.

Tom You see that?

Sophie Very plain.

Tom But you can't. You just *can't*—because it's here—my head.
It's in here!

Sophie And for me it is *there*! Mister, you can lock nothing
away. Time that happened once for you, happens *now* for
me. Why did he do that, your father? To stop you being a
musician? To hurt you?

Tom suddenly stops short: struck by something

Maybe I should stop now?

Tom No. Go on. What else do you see?

Sophie (*addressing herself again to the ball*) You left home in the
North, came to London.

Tom (*in a dead voice*) Boxing Day. Lunch in Euston Station.
Veal and ham pie!

Sophie But you were fortunate in your friends. Recent time has
been good for you. The ball is golden . . . (*Peering harder*) But
now . . . (*Recoiling*) *Oh!*

Tom What?

Sophie Not any more. Not golden now. Going!

Tom Can you see anything particular?

Sophie Gold to grey. Dark. Now pink in dark. Hair. Pink hair—
no, pink scarf—pink something, running, but into darkness . . .
You have a girl-friend?

He shrugs, then nods

She is in flight. I see her shadow, running in the dark. And
after, another shadow: desire running, too. It's— *You*, I think!
Running! running! one shadow trying to take the other! But
now—another. Ja: comes . . . Oh, it's so confused.

Tom Tell me!

Sophie Ssssh! (*Peering fiercely*) This new shadow is much bigger.
Ja: another man. It grows—swarms up over everything, you
and her both—enormous red shadow up over everything!
Over the grey, over the pink, over the dark, the red—the—
red, the—*red*—RED!! (*She breaks off with a cry of dis-
tress*)

Tom What is it?

Sophie No!

Tom What?

Sophie (*in a tone of awe*) I have seen it. The blood-flash. I have seen it.

Tom The blood?

Sophie Blood-flash. The most rare vision in divination. Red blood, drowning the ball. I have read about this, but never have I seen it till now, running over the glass . . . It means— the most terrible warning.

Tom Warning?

Sophie You are doing something that is not good, mister. If you continue—disaster will strike at you. Disaster. And very soon. I mean it, mister. I'm sorry.

A pause. Tom lowers his head, as if he is in tears

(*Impressively*) If there is anything in your emotional life which is not what it should be—I beg of you: beware! If there is a girl in your life at the moment, she is not for you . . .!

But she has to break off: Tom is laughing too hard. She stares at him, scandalized

Tom How much did he pay you?

Sophie Pay?

Tom Well, how did he set it up? He must have offered you a few quid on the side. He couldn't have expected you to do it for nothing.

Sophie What do you mean, please?

Tom (*rising, wiping his eyes with his scarf*) All the same, it's fantastic! I mean, what's the point? Is it supposed to be a joke? Fun and games by the sea?

Sophie Mister, are you suggesting I've been bribed?

Tom I'm not suggesting it. I'm saying it.

Sophie How dare you? How absolutely bloody dare you?

Tom Because I absolutely bloody know, that's how. There's only one person in the world I've ever told those things about my childhood. and that's Frank.

Sophie (*loftily*) My dear mister, to a professional eye like mine, Truth does not have to be told. It is evident.

Tom I daresay. And what if it *isn't* the truth?

A long pause

Sophie I beg your pardon?

Tom What if it's a zonking great lie? Like every word of that story?

Sophie I don't believe it.

Tom It's true.

Sophie Impossible. You say this to discredit me.

Tom Why should I do that?

Sophie Look, mister—what I see, I see. Lemberg never lies!

Tom No, but *I do*!

Pause

Sophie You mean—your father is not a miner?

Tom No. He's a very rich accountant living in Leeds. (*He sits again, indolently*)

Sophie And your mother is not dead?

Tom Not in the biological sense, no. She likes her game of golf, and gives bridge parties every Wednesday.

Sophie But your accent!

Tom (*dropping it completely*) I'm afraid that's as put on as everything else. I mean, there's no point changing your background if you're going to keep your accent, now is there?

Sophie Beloved God!

Tom Actually, it slips a bit when I'm drunk, but people just think I'm being affected.

Sophie (*astounded*) You mean to say—you live your whole life like this? One enormous great lie from morning to night?

Tom Yes, I suppose I do.

Sophie *Unimaginable!*

Tom Does it worry you?

Sophie Doesn't it worry you?

Tom Not particularly. I regard it as a sort of . . .

Sophie White lie?

Tom Yes, very good! A white lie . . .

Sophie But why? In heaven's name, why? Why? WHY?

Tom Well, it's a question of image, really. When I was a kid, in pop music you had to be working-class to get anywhere at all. Middle-class was right out. Five years ago no-one believed you can sing with the authentic voice of the people if you're the son of an accountant—and here we are!

Sophie Incredible. And your parents, do they know that you have abolished them completely—like they never existed?

Tom No, but it doesn't matter. They've abolished *me*, after all. How real am I to them? Dad calls me "Minstrel Boy" whenever I go home, because he finds it embarrassing to have a singer for a son. And Mother tells her bridge club I'm in London studying music—because *studying* is a more respectable image for her than performing in a cellar. Both of them are talking about themselves, not me. And that's fine, because that's what everybody's doing all the time, everywhere. Do you dig?

Sophie But at least you've told this girl-friend? She knows the truth?

Tom Sue? No.

Sophie You mean you just go on and on telling her lies about your terrible childhood?

Tom She likes it. She finds it all very sad.

Sophie That's the most disgusting thing I ever heard! Do you think you can borrow suffering—just to make yourself attractive?

Tom I know I can.

Sophie He was right, your friend. You're a monster.

Tom turns. A pause

Tom Is that what he said?

Sophie His word exact. A monster.

Tom (*laughing*) I don't believe it.

Sophie Of course not. All the same, to me it's obvious. I can see it now quite clearly.

Tom As clearly as you saw my past life in that ball?

Sophie Don't be impertinent. Remember, please, who you are speaking to. You are in the presence of a Baroness of the Holy Roman Empire!

Sophie glares at him, wrapping her shawl tighter about her. Bewildered, he goes into the ante-room

Sophie (*calling out, very angry*) There will be no charge!

Tom (*equally upset*) Oh, thank you!

He stands in the ante-room. Hastily Sophie rises and takes a swig from the decanter

Monster? What? I don't get any of this . . .

He returns unexpectedly. She takes the decanter hastily from her lips

I don't understand! What's been going on?

Sophie (*trying to recover her dignity*) Going on?

Tom You tell me!

Sophie Look, mister: it was a joke. Your friend is a joker. He made up this whole thing to amuse you. He said to me life was a bit grim for you at the moment. The engagement here was not so good—you were both down in the mouth. He suggested I cheered you up . . .!

Tom No.

Sophie I assure you.

Tom That's not it.

Sophie Of course it is. Most certainly: what else? Do you imagine I would do such a thing for real? Ja, ja, to amuse, why not? But *seriously*—to betray, my art? *Do you think I would?*

Tom (*working it out*) You had to see disaster for me and Sue. If we—she and me got together . . . He's trying to warn me. Warn me off . . . My God! (*His mouth opens in amazement*)

Sophie So he's jealous. Is that so astounding . . .? He's right to be, isn't he?

Tom What d'you mean?

Sophie Look, I know you, mister. I know you very well. Don't look at me like that—"Oh my God!" "What do you mean?" I'm not ashamed of what I did! I took money under false pretences. Good. Good, good, good—because for a good good purpose.

Tom What are you talking about?

Sophie Please go now. Absolutely at once! There's no point to discuss further. There really isn't . . .

Tom (*alarmed*) Just tell me this, first. How long has he known about me and Sue?

She looks at him sharply

Did he say? A couple of weeks? A month? I mean, Jesus, to be that *hidden*! Not to give one sign. Just wait, day after day—build up and build up—keep your face smiling all the time. And then come down here for the day, pull a stunt lie this—thinking about it all the way down in the van, I suppose . . . I mean, *who is he*?

Sophie A Giver.

Tom What?

Sophie A Giver, mister. Impossible for you to imagine, of course. Someone who just gives, over and over to the end. Hidden, you call him. Of course . . . Just because he's too proud to show the pain he feels. He is now walking by the sea asking that same question about you: "*Who is he?* What does he want? I gave him everything. Admiration. Not enough. Security. Not enough. I take him out of a slum—absolutely broke—give him my own flat to share, not one penny in rent—not enough! I make him a job. A whole Group I form for him. White satin—engagements—everything so he can fulfil his talent, not just sing for pennies in a filthy pub."

Tom He told you *that*?

Sophie Ja, mister, he told me. The poor idiot. He doesn't know about people like you. Take and take and take until the cows are at home. Take his hope, take his happiness—everything—everything you find!

Tom (*breaking*) Here, I'm off!

Sophie Ja, run! Run! The truth is unbearable, isn't it?

Tom The what?

Sophie The truth. *The truth*, mister! It's a meaningless word to you, isn't it?

A pause. Tom stands by the door, controlling himself. Sophie stands by the table, breathing heavily

Tom (*quietly*) All right. Just for the record, for the record, that's all—I'll give you three straight facts. Then I'll go. I met him. I wasn't broke. I wasn't living in a slum. And I'd formed my group a good year before I set eyes on him.

Sophie The White Liars.

Tom That's right.

Sophie White Liars, *liars* is right!

Tom (*protesting*) We had a regular gig every Friday at the Iron

Duke in the Commercial Road! You can check on that, if you like.

Sophie Black liars! Black! Not white!

Tom (*insistently*) He used to come every weekend with Sue, and sit in the corner listening to us. I just remember eyes—his brown ones and her big blue ones—and they'd sit there and groove on us for hours, just like they were the only people in the world who knew about us. Yeh—that's it! Like we were simply part of their private world, with no existence anywhere else . . .

He comes back into the room. She is suddenly listening

Then suddenly one night, about six months ago, he comes over to me—says his name's Frank—he's a freelance journalist, and wants to do a whole story on The Liars for one of the Sunday Papers. What they call a Study in Depth. It'll mean living around us for a while—did I mind? Well, it sounded great to me. I said fine. And there it was. I mean that's how it all began—with me chasing publicity! . . . A whole month— no, longer—he just followed us about, *observing*. Endless notes in a little book. Always grinning. Silly, you know, but very likeable. He was a mad talker: you couldn't stop him, for anything. I used to tell him, a journalist is supposed to listen, not yap all the time, but he'd just laugh. "I like talking," he'd say: "It's the best thing in the world, after eating." I was living out in Winchmore Hill then, with my Aunt Daisy. Too much glazed chintz, but definitely not a slum. The only kind of music she likes is the sort you can chew tea-cakes to. In the end I left and moved in with him. I hadn't been there a week before I discovered he owed three months' rent.

Sophie No!

Tom Which I paid.

Sophie I don't believe you.

Tom And a week after that, I found out he wasn't really a journalist at all. He worked with Sue in a boutique in the King's Road.

Sophie That's not true.

Tom Till he was sacked.

Sophie You're making it up.

Tom Why should I do that? Look, can't you dig? From the

moment Frank came in here he handed you a pack of lies. One after another.

Frank returns, comes down the stairs and enters the ante-room

Sophie Fibs, maybe. That's possible.

Tom Lies.

Sophie Stories.

Tom *Lies!* Zonking great lies!

Sophie (*suddenly furious*) All right, lies, so what? *So what?* So he did, so he tells a couple of—of tales just to make himself a little more important—You dare! *You* dare talk about liars! You, with your coal mines, guitar on the fire—your whole disgusting childhood!

Tom *His!*

Sophie What?

Tom *His! His* lies! All of them

Sophie *His* lies. About *your* childhood?

Tom (*more softly*) His and hers together. Theirs.

Gulls and wind are heard. Frank, standing by the curtain in the ante-room, listens intently

Sophie (*carefully*) Mister, I don't know what the hell you are saying.

Tom If I said they'd made me up, would you get it? If I said, they'd made *me* make me up. That's nearer . . . I don't know. Sometimes I see it, just for a second, a bit of it. Then it clouds over, just like in your ball—and becomes a nightmare . . . (*He moves slowly to the crystal-ball on the table*) If only that thing really worked. If it could really show why. Why things happen.

Sophie That's what it does, mister.

Tom Yes, but to me. (*He picks the ball up*) If I had the gift—just for five minutes to see the whole thing—her and him and me . . . How does it work? Colours, isn't it? Red for rage, black for death? What for fake? Brown? That's good. Butch brown: the sound of my accent, the phoney Yorkshire I put on when I came South, mainly because I couldn't stand my own voice. (*In a Yorkshire accent*) Butch brown! Colour of the moors . . . !

Frank reacts, startled. Tom sits at the table, holding the ball

   (*Dropping the accent*) My grandpa used to talk like that, much

to my mother's shame: I worked it up from him. It's what first
turned them on: especially Frank. He used to sit on the end
of my bed with his pencil and notebook, just grooving on it.
Bogus journalist interviewing bogus miner! "You're so lucky,"
he'd say: "so lucky to be born a Prole. The working-class is
the last repository of instinct." I'd just shrug in my flannel
pyjamas. Shrugs are perfect. You can imply anything with a
good shrug: repository of instinct—childhood misery—Whatever's wanted. (*He sets down the ball*) What colour's that?
The want? The crazy want in someone for an image to turn
him on? Yeh—and the crazy way you play to it, just to make
him feel good. Green, I bet you. Green for nausea . . . (*Simply*)
I watched him make up my childhood. "Where were you
born?" he'd ask me. Then right away, he'd answer himself.
"Some Godawful little cottage in the North, I suppose: no
loo, I suppose, no electric light, I suppose." "I suppose"
meaning "I want". And me, I'd shrug. Shrug, shrug: up goes
his slum. Shrug, shrug: down comes Dad's belt: ow! Anything. I made bricks out of shrugs. Slagheaps. Flagellant
fathers and blanketless winters, and stolen crusts gnawed in
the outside lav! His eyes would pop. "My God, how we treat
kids in this country!" Hers, too—Sue's: no hers were worse.
They'd brim with tears. She was the world's champion brim-
mer! She cried the first night we ever . . .

*Frank gives a start; his hand flies up to his mouth; he strains to
hear more. Tom rises and grows more urgent*

She had this flat on her own, right near the boutique. One night
I'd been over for spaghetti, and I'd played a bit to her after.
Suddenly—chord of E major still fading into the Chelsea
drizzle—she's looking down at me, and her voice is all panty.
"You were born with that," she says. "There's the natural
music of working-people in your hands!" And down comes
her hair—a curtain of buttermilk over my mouth. And there
it is. The want. I know it right away; the same want as his,
all desperate under her hair—"Give it me. An image. Give me
an image! Turn me on!" What do you do? Buttermilk hair
across your aching mouth, what do you do? Mouth opens—
starts to speak—how can you stop it? (*In his Yorkshire accent*)
"You *understand*", it says, dead sincere. "Christ, you under-

stand! . . . I'll tell you. The only encouragement my dad ever gave me was to throw my guitar on the fire. It wasn't much of an instrument, of course, but it was all I could afford . . ." (*Dropping the accent*) Oh green! Green for nausea! And blue, blue, blue for all the tears in her sky—dropping on me! Spattering me! Lashing the Swedish rug like rain on a Bank Holiday beach! I was soaked. I really was. I went to bed with her to get dry. Honest.

A slight pause. Tom starts to walk about the room. His voice betrays increasingly more desperation. Frank stands rigid now. The light has faded considerably

That was three months ago. When did he find out? *She* didn't tell him. She wouldn't dare . . . He guessed. Well, of *course* he guessed! They know each other completely. They *are* each other! . . . Yes.

A pause. Tom and Sophie look at each other

Once I'd spoken—actually spoken a lie out loud—I was theirs. They got excited, like lions after meat, sniffing about me, drooling. I suppose I could have stopped it any time. Just by using my own voice—telling them who I was. But I didn't. Colour the ball yellow. I told myself I didn't want to hurt them. But why not? Who was I? I didn't exist for them. I don't *now*! (*Excitedly*) They want *their* Tom: not me. Tom the idol. Tom the Turn-on. Tom the Yob God born in a slum, standing in his long-suffering, maltreated skin—all tangled hair and natural instinct—to be hung by his priests in white satin! Yeh: that's the real colour for it all. *White.* Our uniform for The Liars. He designed it—she made it—I wear it! You should see me in it! Frothy white lace round the working-class throat! (*In his Yorkshire accent*) "I look right handsome in it!"

Sophie (*crying out*) Stop it, now, mister! Stop it! Words on words on words on words. What *he* did—what *she* did—what *they* did! And all to escape the guilt of what *you* did!

Tom I?

Sophie Of course, you! *You* told the lies, didn't you? *You* needed the worship. The fact remains, Mr Taker, he gave you everything he had.

Tom He gave me a role, that's what he gave! Can't you see that?
I'm just acting in a film projected out of their eyes. "I Was A
Prisoner On Wet Dream Island!"

Sophie Oh, ha, ha, ha. Very funny! The truth is much simpler
than that, mister. Simpler and much more nasty.

Tom Is it?

Sophie A boring, familiar, nasty old story! You had a friend.
He had a girl. You stole her. And that's all. (*Pause*) Actually
he has not guessed you have been sleeping with her three
months. He just feared you might, one day soon . . . It's why
he came here with his stupid game. Poor fellow. Poor stupid
fellow . . . Ja, but people in love do many desperate things.
You wouldn't understand that, of course. Good-bye, mister.

A pause

Tom (*simply*) Love, you really are in the wrong business, aren't
you?

Sophie What do you mean?

Tom Excuse me.

Tom goes out suddenly into the ante-room

Sophie (*calling after him*) What do you mean, please?

Tom sees Frank standing there, in the gloom. Frank is very upset

Tom How long have you been there?

Frank Few minutes.

Sophie (*to herself*) Beloved God! (*She stands rigidly, trying to
listen*)

Tom You heard.

Frank No. No. Nothing . . . Heard what? I—I—I've just this
second come in . . .

Tom Good-bye, Frank.

Tom goes out of the ante-room and on to the Pier

Frank Where are you going? Tom!

Frank follows Tom outside

Where are you going?

Tom (*in a very posh accent*) Back to Lichfield, old boy—back
home.

Frank No! You can't . . . All right, it was disgusting—it was a
  stupid bloody trick: I'm sorry. It was plain awful, I know—I
  know. But you just can't go like this. You can't just go!

Tom What else would you suggest?

Frank Well, we could—we could—surely we . . .

Tom I've had it, Frank. With you. With her. With me, actually.
  You were right about one thing. The word you used. "Monster."

Frank I didn't mean that.

Tom You should.

Frank That was the heat of the moment!

Tom Tara, Frank. (*He puts out his hand*)

Frank Tom, please. Can't we talk about this?

*Tom shakes his head, smiles awkwardly, then suddenly turns and
runs up the steps and out of sight*

(*Calling after him*) Tom! You've got the concert! (*Howling
suddenly*) TOM!

*He stands still. Gulls and wind. Then slowly he goes back inside.
Sophie has seen Tom running away. Now she hears Frank return
and stand in the ante-room*

Sophie Mister—Mister, won't you come in here, please?

*Frank stays where he is. She addresses him, unseen, from the
darkening parlour*

I'm sorry. It's not gone so well, our little trick. It exploded,
didn't it? I'm afraid that is sometimes the way with tricks . . .
Still, it's not so bad, is it? After all, it's what you wanted
really—him to go away. "Make him go", you asked me. "Get
rid of him for me." Well, I can't claim I did it myself, but it's
been done, mister. He's gone. You won't see him again. It's
not such a bad day's work, after all. Your girl is quite safe
now: that's the important thing.

A faint sob comes from the ante-room

Mister? *Mister . . .?*

The sobs grow louder. Frank is in agony. Sophie moves across the parlour to the ante-room, draws the curtain and enters it. Frank turns away from her

Oh come now, please. I don't understand.
Frank No, you don't, do you?
Sophie You wanted him to go.

He turns on her

Frank I wanted him to leave her alone! . . . And to stay with me. In—my—bed.

She stares at him

He'd been there six months.

A pause. Slowly Sophie retreats from the ante-room, back into the parlour. She stands by the curtain, deeply upset

Sophie He's right, your friend. I'm in the wrong business. I see nothing. I understand nothing, any more. I'm in the wrong place. The wrong world. *Who are you all?* You weird people— you young, weird, mad people! I was brought up in a proper world. People were clear, what they were—what they wanted! People were decent! I don't understand this world now— freaks and frauds and turn me on! I don't understand *anything anymore*! It's all so ugly! (*She grows more and more desperate*) I was born into a world of order and beauty! That's what it meant to be noble—to give order to the world, and beautiful things. Not just tummy-twisting and wow-wow-wow like sick dogs! There was beauty, mister. My father brought me up in beauty, to respect beauty—to respect *people*—not make jokes of them—not dress like lunatics and make fun of people! I knew the Old World, mister! I knew the real world! My father, he knew the real world! He taught me how to live—my father; he taught me beauty—he taught me truth—he knew everything, my father—beauty and music and loving—he knew everything, everything—he knew NOTHING!

With a sudden swipe she smashes the photograph off the table on to the floor. Frank is startled by the noise. She stares at the picture with hatred. Her speech gets more and more upset, but does not lose rapidity

Weak, stupid little man! Folded his hands in front of the world, and said nothing. Just nothing! Every day on the twenty-seven bus, for fourteen years. Eight forty-five leave the house, back at seven smelling of gherkins! Gherkins have a smell, mister— you know that smell? The smell of delicatessens? I said he was what to you? A baron? Don't believe it. Take comfort, mister—here's a bit of comfort. It's not only the young who lie, whatever I said, it's not true—the old are worse. They are the biggest liars of them all! He was not a baron; I am not a baroness; my mother was not a Romany noblewoman, she was just a gypsy—and not even interesting. Just a quarter-gypsy, not colourful with scarves and lovers—just dull. Dull lady, always frightened. Both of them, always frightened! He had no estates, my dear: his estate was a Kosher delicatessen in the town of Innsbruck. After Hitler, he worked exactly at the same trade in London. Gherkins in Innsbruck, gherkins in Crawford Street—the Prater Deli: Proprietor Harry Plotkin. That is my real name: *Plotkin!* I started the fortune-telling because I could not bear to stand behind a counter and spoon out pickles! My mother said "it's beneath you to tell fortunes." *Beneath!* Do you hear? Better of course to ladle out gherkins all your life into little cartons! "Thank you, madame, that will be two pounds forty . . . Thank you, sir! Thank you, thank you!"

Frank suddenly makes a move: he cannot bear any more. He starts for the door—suddenly he notices the toy dog. He picks it up

The photograph you saw, that is a costume. (*She takes the crystal-ball, recovers it and carries it back to its shelf*) The Paddington Opera Society presented *The Count of Luxembourg*, and my father got into the chorus. I found the medals myself for him, in the Portobello Road. They are not exactly accurate.

Frank walks slowly out of the door, and away up the stairs, holding the dog. He disappears into the evening

Sophie does not realize he has left. She kneels down and picks up the photograph. Her speech grows a little more tender but no slower

One thing I told you was true. His clarinet. After he came here he never touched it: but in Austria he played quite well. And there *was* a lake. It wasn't ours, but we went there every year, two weeks in the summer, and stayed at a Guest House on the shore. One year the Rosé Quartet was staying there also for a couple of nights, appearing at the Salzburg Festival. And one evening, for a quarter of an hour, they let him play with them: the slow movement of the Brahms. I sat on a chair on the grass. I watched him. He looked unbelievable. He narrowed his eyes behind his pince-nez, and he concentrated everything inside him, and he made no mistakes at all. Not one. They let him play the whole movement. And just as he finished the sun went down, just like that, went absolutely out like a light, exactly as if it had been arranged. And that was the best moment of his life . . . (*She gets up, and replaces the photograph. She is half crying*) Well, well, well: other years, other tears . . .

The lights on the pier suddenly come on: a bright string of little bulbs. She raises her voice in the gloom, to the ante-room

Why are you crying, mister? For *whom*? Your lover? What lover? There never *was* one! *Who did you lose, you stupid boy?* You hear me, mister? You want my advice? Advice and Consultation! Go home now—go home and find someone *real*! That's my advice to you, mister—and it's good. It's the best. I tell you something: *Plotkin Never Lies!* Do you hear me, mister? That's my joke for today. *Plotkin Never Lies!* (*She pours herself a drink*) That's my joke for tomorrow.

Gulls and wind. Sophie salutes the gulls with her glass, and drinks. The Light fades on her, into darkness, as—

the CURTAIN *falls*

FURNITURE AND PROPERTY LIST

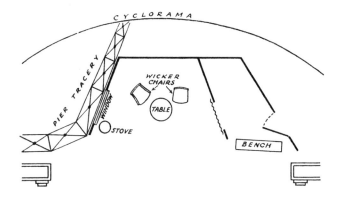

On stage: Circular table. *On it:* cloth, fan, bottle of gin, funnel, rose-coloured decanter, rose-coloured wineglass, playing-cards set out, card of charges, pencil, photograph in silver frame. *Below it:* wastepaper basket
2 broken-down chairs
Rusty oilstove
Strip of carpet
On shelf at back: crystal-ball under covering
In ante-room: bench

Off stage: Large woolly dog (**Tom**)

Personal: **Frank:** coin, envelope with notes, 10 one-pound notes
Tom: scarf, 3 one-pound notes

LIGHTING PLOT

Property fittings required: hanging-lamp (dressing only), string of
coloured "Pier" lights

Interior. A booth and ante-room

To open: Effect of late autumn, 5 p.m.

Cue 1	**Tom:** "... the first night we ever ..." *Start fade to dusk*	(Page 26)
Cue 2	**Sophie:** "... other years, other tears ..." *Snap on coloured Pier lights*	(Page 32)
Cue 3	**Sophie** drinks *Fade to Black-out for* CURTAIN	(Page 32)

EFFECTS PLOT

Cue 1	As **Sophie** pours gin *Seagulls scream*	(Page 1)
Cue 2	**Tom:** "His and hers together. Theirs." *Seagulls and wind*	(Page 25)
Cue 3	**Frank:** ". . . the concert. TOM!" *Seagulls and wind*	(Page 29)
Cue 4	**Sophie:** ". . . my joke for tomorrow." *Seagulls and wind*	(Page 32)

MADE AND PRINTED IN GREAT BRITAIN BY
LATIMER TREND & COMPANY LTD PLYMOUTH

MADE IN ENGLAND